The $50 Startup Guide:

7 online businesses you can start today

Table of Contents

Introduction

First things first, I need to thank you for purchasing this book. You guys are the reason I create these titles with the hopes of helping all of you break the mold of a 9-5 job, working hard every day so that you can provide for your loved ones while someone you may never have even met, gets rich.

I would also like to congratulate you for your purchase because, in this book you will learn 7 ways to break the mold and build wealth for yourself. It all starts by being able to supplement your income. These 7 side hustles are not just any businesses that can operate online, what good would that be for you? They all have two things in common. One, they are all very profitable. And two, you can launch, from start to finish, with less than $50. I know, crazy talk. But no. People just like you and I are doing it every day. They just recognized an opportunity in the market and capitalized on it.

As we explore these 7 basic businesses to launch fast and cheap, just ask yourself, what do you really have to lose by risking $50 on the chance to make an endless amount? I say endless because there really is no cap or limit to how much revenue you are allowed to generate. That is for you to decide with your time, effort, and marketing ability.

If you take away only one thing from this book, then it has paid for itself with the new knowledge you have. Will you turn this knowledge into cash, or just continue on without?

Without the chance to reach to true potential. Fortune favors the bold. We've all heard that once or twice, and it couldn't be more true. No one ever made riches by playing it safe. No 24-year-old is retiring because their mutual fund just exploded by 10,000 times his investment. However, many are in fact 'retiring' at that age by mining their own business. We have all heard the saying, mind your own business. Maybe the saying really means, mine your own business. Such as starting a business and working for yourself. But what kind? Where do I start? What am I even good at? I'll help you find the answers to those questions here, in this guide. I bet by now the excitement must be excruciating right? So without any further delay, let's get started!

Fiverr gigs

This is a short one to explain. Fiverr is a website where anyone can join for free and create a job posting of something they will do for $5. You then have the option to sell upgrades, packages, and other extra gigs for a price you choose through a drop down menu. This ranges from $5 - $990, though the average is $25 - $55. You can create a gig for just about anything, even making a prank call. Many people have generated over $50,000 a year and have moved full time with Fiverr. With millions of visitors every day, it's no wonder people who can get traffic to their gigs are having great success. E.g. If you can sell 10 gigs per day with an average price of $15 each, you will have generated over $54,000 in yearly sales. I've had someone pay me just under $80 to email one of his buddies as a woman and ask to meet him at a local bar (where the friend that hired me would be waiting), easy money! The best part is that you can do this, and every other business mentioned within these pages, from home and on your own time. Especially since Fiverr allows you to create custom delivery deadlines for your orders. Now how long would you have to work for your boss to generate $54,000 in annual income? Of which, is then taxed heavily by the government. Unearned income (money made by side businesses) is taxed at a lower percentage than the money you make working at a traditional job.

If you have a special skill and/or you are creative, then this following story might be something that is of interest for you, whilst also being extremely profitable. A post from the Fiverr blog follows the story of Katie, a Fiverr seller. She was looking to leave her full-time job but just needed some way to supplement her income. She looked to Fiverr as a way to leverage her talent as a voiceover artist. I must say that, with now over 10,000 completed orders resulting in over $100,000 in revenue, she is doing a great job. She has reached this achievement by striving for 100% customer satisfaction, social media promotions, and being personable with her customers.

Fiverr arbitrage

If you are interested in Fiverr gigs that we mentioned before but are looking for something a little more passive, then Fiverr arbitraging may be of interest to you. What it consists of is setting up a website that offers a service that someone on Fiverr is also offering. You keep the difference of what they charge and what you sell it for. Like a wholesaler or middleman of sorts. Here is an example of a business that you can create very cheap, and very fast. Now about that logo design company. Let's say you create a website for your logo company. Design the website using super easy, user-friendly, services like WordPress. Once its looking up to your standards and you've create different packages to sell. Starting with a beginner package and ending at an executive package, with a professional package being in the middle. Once your site is live to the public and you've used various ways to generate traffic to your site, you just wait for an order to come in. While you wait for online orders, I highly recommend you start calling around various small businesses in your local area and inquire as to if they are interested in a logo redesign. Inform them that you are running a special right now at the low price of (your highest package price) for our highest quality, Executive Package. Keep in mind that your highest price should still be well below the industry average for the job you're doing, since your overhead is substantially lower. Having 800-1,000% profit margins shouldn't be farfetched but if they bulk at the price you can reassure them that you stand by your quality and un-matched turnaround speed on designs. If they are still not interested in the highest package, and they offer legitimate reasons as to why. Such as, it may be overkill for what they need or things of that nature. You can direct them to your smaller packages that you offer (with 800-1000% margins on each package, you can make a handsome profit selling any of them), leading with the professional package and stating that it is your most popular among some of your more successful customers. This should help them over the fence if they we stuck on it. Starting out as a One-Man Army at first is a good way to insure a profit when grinding out sales. So, you got the sale. Now you go over to Fiverr and find a highly rated, 5-star logo designer by searching "Logo Design" in the Fiverr search bar. You then simply gather the information about the needs and wants for the logo you received from your customer and pass it along to your Fiverr designer. Some will allow you to purchase expedited delivery within 24hrs for an additional fee. The equivalent to your Executive Package can be bought from you on Fiverr for around $90-250. The other packages costing much less, $5-55. Once they submit a design to you for review, you pass it along to your customer for their review. Request that they get back to you as soon as possible. This is so you can finalize the design with your Fiverr designer more quickly. If they request a revision to the logo, then contact your Fiverr designer and ask them for the same redesign instructions that the customer submits to you. Most will offer at least one free revision. Many will offer up to 5 revisions of the design and also provide other additions such as transparency's, digital rights, source file, etc. included in their packages. While you're able to sell your logo design packages to companies for over $2,500 each, you can see where getting only one or two customers per month can equate to a nice side income for most people. 10 customers would be even nicer! I mean who doesn't like over 1000% profit margins on something with low overhead. Once again, this is a business you can run from anywhere you can get an internet connection. Which is most places in the world today. Even in the more rural countries.

I, for one, love the idea of running my business from a Wi-Fi connection on the beach. The truth is that there are countries that you can do just that. In fact, some places you can live like a king with a large home with staff and maid services for $800-900USD per month. Other countries you can live even cheaper than that. For instance, if you find the right locals and avoid tourist avenues then for $190USD per month you can live in beautiful Mumbai, India or gorgeous San Juan del Sur, Nicaragua. There are so many places you can do this at as well. These are just examples of what you can achieve with internet businesses that continue to make USD while you live in a place that allows you to spend a currency that exchanges at a much lower rate.

e-Commerce Shop

Starting up your own e-commerce shop is probably the most lucrative business we will cover in this guide. With low startup cost, there has already been hundreds of thousands of million dollar businesses established on the internet from average joes like you and me. I'm going to cover a few of these businesses to show you the potential of a simple e-commerce store. Many of which built their websites on platforms such as Shopify, BigCommerce, etc. which allows you to build an ecommerce style website using templates and plug-ins without knowing how to write a single line of code. Using these services, you can register a domain name and they will also host your site included in a monthly fee based on the package you select.

An example of a company that has made some serious dough using one of these platforms, we will discuss, The Pink Lilly Boutique. They moved their site to the BigCommerce platform, with no transaction fees, this platform is a powerful tool for beginners. This husband and wife team wanted to start their own successful online fashion boutique, and they accomplished just that. By moving over to this new platform, they posted a gain of 40% increase in revenues and daily visitors amounting to just under 20k, with orders reaching over 600 per day. The Pink Lilly

Boutique now has over 1 million followers on social media with over $1 million in sales annually.

Another wildly successful e-commerce site is one that you may recognize. Zappos. Zappos, originally an online shoe retailer that changed the way e-commerce shops do business by offering free shipping, including returns and a 365-day return period. This allowed them to gain popularity very quickly among customers and gained the attention of Amazon. Amazon acquired Zappos in 2009 for $1.2 billion. Headquartered in Las Vegas with less than 2,000 employees, and branching out into more than just shoes. Zappos now sells all sorts of clothing for men, woman, and children alike, resulting in $2 billion in revenue annually. Not too shabby for an online store.

Founder and ex-CEO of Nasty Girl, Sophia Amoruso started her business in 2006 as an eBay shop. Nasty Girl has grown astronomically over the last 10 years and has posted year over year growth of 500% in its early years before flattening out over the last few years. With a consistent $100 million in annual sales, Sophia has grown an amazing business for herself. Sophia stepped down as CEO in January of 2015 to focus on the creativity side of Nasty Girl. With the hopes of this change in focus and job title for Ms. Amoruso, Nasty Girl can grow into an even larger e-commerce monster than it currently is.

These examples just go to show you how fast and how profitable an e-commerce store can truly be if you have an understanding on how to run and market your business as well as persistence to see it pay off.

Blogging

Blogging, blogging, blogging. Blogging has been one of the most well-know, most attempted, and one of the oldest forms of making money on the modern day internet. It can also be one of the most difficult and time consuming. The hardest part is building a following with interesting and exciting content that will drive visitors to your site. Once you have a following however, the possibilities are endless. Various ways to make income from your blog include; affiliate commissions, PPC ads, CPM ads, CPA ads, private ads, banner ads, product sales, and charging a membership fees. I will cover a few examples of successful blogs below.

The first we will cover is The Huffington Post. Created by Arianna Huffington, the Huffington Post grew in popularity and was eventually sold to AOL is 2011 for $315 million. The Huffington Post generates income via PPC ads or pay per click advertising. This is where they post ads to their site and are paid when their visitors click on the ads there are showing. When the site was sold it generated over $2.3 million monthly, or just under $28 million annually. In 2014, the site generated $146 million in revenue. It is said that Arianna walked from the deal with only $21 million. Still, no small number for most of us but less than 7% of the sale price after brokers fees, etc.

Pat Flynn, creator and owner of the Smart Passive Income blog generated $1.4 million in 2015 and is on track to bring in more than $2.1 million in 2016. Pat Flynn grew his site to be extremely popular by his visitors and growing following by remaining very transparent in the amount of revenue his sites generate. Even at the time of the publication of this guide, Pat shows his monthly income for the previous months right in the header of his site and members get emails monthly updating them on the amount of ad revenue he has generated. With only him and a small team running his business, it is very profitable.

The last blog we will discuss before moving on will be Life Hacker. Life Hacker, founded by Gina Trapani and launched in 2005, is currently owned by Gawker Media. Life Hacker, who creates post about making your life easier through different "hacks" if you will. It is estimated that in 2014, Life Hacker generated close to $2.4 million.

These examples are just three of many thriving blogs that exists in the vast entity that is the internet. If you can consistently pump out interesting material, then you may be leaving money on the table by not starting your own blog. Or maybe one of the other businesses we discuss is more your speed. Let's move on.

Podcasting

Podcasting has exploded into a massive market and is only showing signs of growing, and growing quickly at that. Many entrepreneurs are making major incomes from this form of an internet business. Even many celebrities have moved to hosting their own podcast to make money. In this section, we won't be discussing such podcast. Instead, we will be focusing on successful podcast that have been started by average people like you and I.

One of the companies we will be covering is the TWiT.tv company. This company was founded by Leo Laporte and started out as the This Week in Tech podcast and has since grown to over 20 different podcast all owned by the TWiT LLC umbrella company. Although the company is owned by Leo, his wife, Lisa Laporte is the CEO. In 2009, Leo Laporte announced a net profit of $1.2 million. Clearly, this husband and wife team works extremely well together. TWiT also announced that they estimate they will generate $7 million in fiscal 2015. With an estimated $1.6 million in cost, that would leave Leo and Lisa with $5.4 million in net profits. Including live events and all other various forms of income generated by the company, it is said TWiT grossed $8 million in 2013 alone. With the flagship show, This Week in Tech, averaging $50,000 per weekly episode and having over 20 shows on your network can really add up to some serious profits.

Another successful podcaster is also a youtuber. Shane and Friends was created Shane Dawson and Lauren Schnipper in 2013. The show was an instant success as it jumped to the #125 spot on iTunes within 24hrs of its launch. Lauren Schnipper, who was also his producer, soon after left the show to seek other opportunities and has been replaced by Jessie Buttafuoco. With an estimated $15,250 in revenue per episode and 20 episodes listed in 2015, Shane and Friends would have generated over $300,000 just by selling advertising on their episodes. If, in 2016, Shane and Friends makes no additional revenue from any source other than strictly selling advertising slots. Let's say they increase their content upload to once per week, for a total of 52 episodes. This business model alone would result in a total of $793,000 in revenue being generated. Or, an additional $488,000 than previously generated in 2015.

The sky is really the limit when it comes to building a brand and a business online. If we just quickly touch on another podcasting business as an example, we will talk about Epic Meal Time. Have you ever heard of them? Well Harley and the crew over at EMT have supplemented their income by selling their own branded food spreads, t-shirts, and other things. Many other companies, usually run by an individual in a company branded around their name, will do live events and seminars to make additional revenue. Sometimes they consider this form of revenue as their own personal income and not revenue generated by the business itself.

eBooks

Many of the businesses discussed within this short guide require a skill of sorts but eBooks are something that only requires knowledge. Knowledge about almost any topic can be incredibly successful and profitable. There are countless examples of entrepreneurs and unintended millionaires making it big from self-publishing their own eBooks. Many of these individuals are living like kings on a foreign beach somewhere. With eBooks growing in popularity and the future looking more and more towards mobile applications, electronic books, and magazines, the popularity is only going to rise. The fact that once you create an eBook product and put it out to market, it will always be there and therefore can continue to make you sales in perpetuity; or in other words, FOREVER. Between iBooks, Kindle Marketplace, and other large digital publishing services, you can get your product in front of millions and millions of potential customers while collecting anywhere from 35%-85% royalty commissions per sale.

Self-published author Mark Dawson reportedly rakes in $450,000 thanks to amazon's kindle direct publishing. Dawson stated that he cleared six figures but never discloses exact figures. However, knowing the royalty commission plans on amazon will allow us to speculate. We can estimate that, using the 70% royalty plan and the gross revenue of $450,000 leaves Mark with around $315,00 in gross profits. After taxes, assuming a 35% tax rate, Mr. Dawson would be left with around $204,000 net profit.

As I mentioned before, you can sell it forever as long as it remains relevant. Perhaps you'll have to make updates to your products every couple years to bring it up to date, but $200,000 annually should be adequate motivation. Once you create an eBook, you can sell it on your own personal website for an even lower price than amazon and make a higher profit by receiving more than 90-95% after figuring in payment processor fees. Websites like createspace.com will allow you to upload your word doc to their site and it will automatically format your book for kindle. Once its formatted and your cover photo is created and approved (you can upload your own as well), you can publish to kindle and also have the opportunity to sell a paper version of your book on-demand for a higher price than kindle will allow digital version to be sold, while maintaining an 85% royalty commission per sale. They also offer buyer to purchase the digital copy for 2.99 or less if they purchased your paper copy at some point.

Many eBooks end up making the New York Times Bestsellers list. Some of these titles include the extremely popular titles such as: Think and Grow Rich, by Napolean Hill. Rich Dad, Poor Dad, by Robert Kiyosaki. The 4-Hour Work Week, by Timothy Ferriss. Of which, all have inspired many and changed the way they approach their life and outlook on it as well. Another great title such as, The Millionaire Fastlane, by MJ DeMarco describes scenarios in which he gives examples of what he calls both the Fastlane and the Slowlane, respectively. Have you ever heard; graduate from college, get a good job, save 10-15% of your paychecks into a 401(k), pinch pennies, trust the stock market, work hard until you're 65, retire, and hope the government takes care of the rest? This book will discuss why that's the Slow lane and MJ DeMarco will discuss the Fastlane and why it isn't out of reach for you, while also giving you examples of the Fastlane. It's both eye-opening and exciting to read, or listen to. He also has an audible version of the book, as do the other mentioned in this section. Pick those up for some good reads while at work or driving to and from.

Udemy Course

Udemy is a service where you can create and teach your own course about just about anything. You set the fee to purchase your class or course and drive traffic to it for optimum results. One story we will discuss is about a young man who marketing his course in a clever and cheap way. Since the launch of Udemy, many individuals have turned large profits. Some generate over a million annually. Once you finish with the work and effort it takes to complete a successful and valuable course and get it uploaded to Udemy, the work is done. You can then constantly generate income regardless of where you are or if you are sleeping or not. The money pours in.

Take it from Walter. He took to Udemy with his course "Swift – Learn Apple's New Programming Language Step by Step". The inspiration came when he attended an Apple development conference in 2013 where the Swift language was introduced. Seeing opportunity, he got straight to work creating a 50 video course after consuming as much knowledge about the new matter as he could and regurgitating the information into his videos. After the course was available it didn't take long before it found success. With over 8,000 students having taken his course and more to certainly follow, his idea is surely a major success.

Until he makes a new course for a new programming language and does this whole thing all over again, who knows, perhaps it will be even more successful than the last.

Walter also launched another class entitled "How to Make a Freaking iPhone App". He created a Kickstarter campaign and began to pre-sell the course marked down from $199 to only $29. It was a huge success. With a campaign goal of only $1,000, he managed to generate more than $66,000 in just one month. Well-done sir, well-done.

Conclusion

We've come to the end of this guide and I hope you've taken away some quality information and maybe some inspiration into an online business idea for yourself. The reason I created this guide and others like it is to distribute information that may spark something within yourself. Something that could inspire you to launch your own business or side hustle. Even if it isn't something specifically covered in this guide, perhaps you thought of a skill you have that you could market and sell online via your own website or a 3rd party platform like some of the ones discussed within these pages.

 Money really can be easy to generate for those whom have value to offer, to those who seek to have it. This could be information, a physical product, or digital product, etc. If you are an expert on something or could be considered one based on the knowledge you have on the subject, then you can probably make money online with that knowledge. With WordPress making it so easy for people who have no knowledge on how to code, build professional looking websites, cheaply. There really is no excuse for not taking a stab at an idea you come up with. Who knows? It may end up being a huge success, making you hundreds of thousands or even, hundreds of millions of dollars in revenue.

I would like to take this time to thank you again for purchasing this guide! Without people like you, looking for ways to a better life financially, I would have no one to write various guides for. Not to mention, no one to buy the damn things!

So don't hesitate, get out there and finally start that big idea of yours! You owe it to yourself, and you owe it to your family. Does this actual risk really outweigh the potential reward? You already took a risk purchasing this guide. Go get 'em.

If you would like to check out my guide on how to launch your own t-shirt business, then follow this link below:

http://www.amazon.com/T-Shirt-Entrepreneur-Ricky-Dempsey-ebook/dp/B01CJ4RWNC/ref=sr_1_1?s=books&ie=UTF8&qid=1457145503&sr=1-1&keywords=tshirt+entrepreneur

www.ingramcontent.com/pod-product-compliance
Lightning Source LLC
Chambersburg PA
CBHW021002180526
45163CB00006B/2466